Not Under Law

We wish to thank our dear friend and colleague, Maurice Smith, for all he has taught us on the subject of grace. Having seen the grace of God at work in his life has spurred us on to write so emphatically about the believers' attitude to law.

NOT UNDER LAW

Gerald Coates/Hugh Thompson

Good Reading Limited
London, England

Logos International
Plainfield, New Jersey

ISBN 0 904223 31 0

Printed in Great Britain by
Tonbridge Printers Ltd, Tonbridge, Kent.

Contents

Preface

We must treat as our enemy any idea, however good, that hinders us from knowing God.

What sort of person is he that would gladly strip away the 'good' in his life in order to obtain the 'best'? Surely no-one but the man who honestly hungers after God.

If you are a contented Christian we suggest you leave this book unread. Only those who yearn for the utter reality of a genuine walk with God will benefit from these pages. Others will almost certainly experience confusion and annoyance. The person who is willing to be revolutionized will give up the ideas and practices that mean so much to him in order to 'know Him'. After reading this, such a man will find he wants to talk over with God many aspects of his life.

We have felt an urge to write because we are deeply distressed over the moral state of the average believer. We have been asking ourselves if the run-of-the-mill evangelical truly longs to rank as an overcomer any more than he strives to gain recognition as a champion of the hoopla! May God persuade us out of this 'average' category.

Much of today's preaching neither gloriously blesses nor radically disturbs, being so watered down that if it were poison it could do no harm and if medicine it would never cure. However, the substance of this message will probably hurt. 'Faithful are the wounds of a friend.' But we do not intend to hurt for the sake of hurting. Like the father with his delinquent child across his knee, we have an end in view! God promises through Moses: 'I wound *and* I heal.' We are praying that our faithful Father will bring healing to individuals, even to whole communities, through this publication, for the glory of His great name.

Aware that many readers will react badly through misunderstanding what we have written, we trust God to sort out the results. We here commit to the Spirit of revelation both the contents of the book and the hearts of the readers. Those who want truth more than convenience or popularity will discover Jesus, the mighty God, as He really is.

Gerald Coates/Hugh Thompson

1. Not Under Law

'Sin shall not be master over you, for you are not under law, but under grace.'[1]

'If you are led by the Spirit, you are not under law.'[2] At the root of most present-day social ills lies the fact of man's hatred to all forms of restrictions and law. Increasingly in our Western culture the lawless minorities dominate society with their philosophies and ideals.

As a result parliaments enforce more stringent legislation to counteract the activities of these lawless groups. The rebels, feeling got-at yet again, disrupt society all the more! Now, a careful study of the Scriptures brings to our notice the startling fact that *God does not want His creatures to serve Him under laws of 'do' and 'don't'. He has planned a higher way of living, free from all laws but one,* 'the law of the Spirit of life in Christ Jesus'.

This concept may surprise many born-again, law-keeping believers. Look again at the verses quoted above. Do they not plainly show us that *no Christian should struggle to keep God's laws?* Once it dawns on you that it means what it says, the glorious reality liberates you. This is one aspect of much hidden truth now being rediscovered in our day. A momentous reformation is gathering force; its eruption will cause Luther's reformation to seem like a minor tremor. We unearth the very foundation of the Gospel of Christ when we squarely face the issue of law and grace. The misunderstanding of the Christian's relation to the law causes, we believe, many of the ills of modern christendom. A right appreciation of this blessed truth will shake individuals and whole churches to their roots.

We detect a major structural flaw throughout the whole range of belief and behaviour among us who name the name of Christ. Multitudes of us believe 'off by head' that we are saved by God's grace, but 'off by heart' we mostly get stung into action by a sense of condemnation. By working for God in order to please Him, we belie the grace that saved us.

Everyone found so working for God has put himself under law!

2. Too Much Big Stick

The lack of victory in our churches does not necessarily stem from a lack of commitment by the members, but because they misunderstand what they are committed to, they stumble from failure to failure.

If a person commits himself to constant endeavour to be a better Christian, he dooms himself to failure before he even starts. Yet standard evangelical counsel generally rises no higher than that. Over a period of time the convert gathers—more by intimation than through verbal instruction—that he must try to please God with all his might. Then 'Get moving for God' and 'Become more involved' are laid on top of the burden he is already carrying that he isn't doing enough for God. If he stands in the cinema queue he is haunted by that devastating question he read in the deeper life magazine: 'How would you feel if, when Jesus comes, he finds you in the cinema?' Or, relaxing in his garden, his ear-drums thud relentlessly with the echo of some pulpit exhortation: 'Look at Brother Blank in darkest Africa, worked to death, oughtn't *you* to be doing more?' And under the pressure of it all he 'does some more witnessing' and puts a few more people off! Oh, what error! What a totally unscriptural parody of the life God has purposed for us.

'Now, what can be done about the lives marked by continual defeat despite trying so hard? And what is God's answer to the masses of *un*-committed pew-warming members of our Gospel churches, those whose whole attitude displays the invisible lapel-badge 'Please do not disturb my private life'? ('We can't be backslidden or we wouldn't come to church at all, would we?')

The problem is the same in both types. Because of its basic nature no amount of Bible study, prayer, witnessing, or service will rectify the conditions. In fact, these people are living in a twilight zone of grace and law, understanding neither. They know that by His grace God blotted out their sins, but now they work for God. They wouldn't miss a quiet time, grace before meals, or attendance at church service lest they incur the wrath and condemnation of the Almighty, (not to mention the disapproval of their brethren). Conversely, diligence in such activities merits divine (and human) favour, they reckon. But all of that is as far from the Gospel as Big Ben is from the peak of Mount Everest. For the Gospel is the good news of grace.

3. What is Grace?

Almost every fundamentalist knows that grace means 'unmerited favour'. One dictionary defines it as 'a concession not claimable as one's right'. But of all groups, we evangelicals have become the victims of our self-made culture. We have never thought through the full implication of all our beautiful gospel language. We have despised dead 'ritualism' but have ensnared ourselves in dead 'rut-ualism'—the rut of assuming that everyone understands our gospel when we ourselves have never faced its radical meaning for our own day-to-day living.

Religion in general is founded on law—the law of 'I must do something for God'. Christianity differs completely. God's assessment of our hopelessness ('*You can do nothing for Me*'), plus His offer of hope ('*but I can do something for you*'), *that* spells *grace*. We experience salvation not by believing facts but by enthroning Jesus Christ as Lord of our lives. The testimony, 'God is my salvation'[3] asserts that salvation is a Person and not a series of outworked activities.

4. Is this Your Life?

We rarely hear the 'You do good and God will bless you' theology explicitly preached in Bible-believing churches. Nevertheless, we are persuaded that it causes most of the pressures in the life of the average converted member.

A false start. According to our observation the modern pilgrim's progress follows a fairly routine pattern. The heart of 'the typical convert' trembled with a sense of sin on hearing the Gospel preached. At the front of the auditorium he received pardon through Jesus' precious blood, and eternal life by His risen power. Then 'Lawson' (what more appropriate name?) was quietly but firmly commanded in the enquiry room to join a Gospel-honouring congregation, pray every day, read the Scriptures without fail and take responsibility in the local church. And what was he told about the law?

'You must try to keep the Ten Commandments. If you fail, God's grace will be sufficient,' the counsellor taught him. But a day or two after, and several moral falls later, his pastor assured him, 'Lawson, my dear boy, you cannot hope to keep the law. That is why Jesus died to save you. You will be a sinner till the day you die.'

Thus he was launched on a problematic course by these confused statements. We would as soon construct an Empire State Building on foundation bricks of ice-cream as hope to build a stable Christian character on such uncertain doctrine! Next he had to merit his membership in the chapel. The elders pointed out the biblical requirement of baptism for 'full membership', but not just yet, of course. After all, he may not understand what baptism is all about. (Do you get the impression that converts in New Testament times knew all that much when *they* were baptised?)

After some months of striving to conform he was allowed baptism and, as a reward for good conduct, 'welcomed' into fellowship.

A dangerous principle was thus forced upon him from the start of his church life —namely, 'Prove yourself and God will bless you.'

In reading the New Testament one doesn't sense that apostles and elders treated new disciples with constant caution. But the traffic lights of modern evanglical leadership are forever amber. Young Lawson had now qualified to break bread with the local saints. But having 'blasted off' on this wrong trajectory, his church activity zeroed-in on 'observing' the Lord's Supper in a strained fashion. (Witnessing was also emphasized to balance up his spiritual life.) The poor fellow would go to the weekly communion service emotionally as cold as a cemetery. Although Jesus had enjoined us to 'Remember Me', this new member didn't see anyone in the chapel literally rejoicing in this celebration of Jesus' victory over death, sin and judgement. They all thought the Lord's word had been 'Remember My Death'. 'Examine yourself,' quoted the preacher, 'and so break bread.' And Lawson did examine himself week after week. He *should* have discovered Christ in him— the hope of glory. But believing himself to be a life-long sinner, he expected to find faults and failings.

In the gloomy stillness he would try to conjure up a visual image of the middle cross, the dark sky behind, the mob around the hill. Sunday by Sunday as a mental gymnast he indulged in this form of idolatry and will-worship. No-one had told him that he could show forth Jesus' death and its triumphant accomplishments. He struggled beneath the law of having to feel something religious at a particular hour on the first day of the week. He tried to be thankful. Occasionally success produced the rosy warmth of pride, but normally he sagged into further condemnation because the emotional response didn't happen.

If the devil cannot prevent the sinner's conversion he will intimidate him thereafter and imprison him in introspection. Lawson's attention turned in on himself again and again, instead of considering Jesus and all that He is.

Wallowing in his repeated defeats, our young friend learned from his seniors how to build himself a defence of proof texts to justify his low level of spirituality. 'O wretched man that I am,' was a good excuse. After all, the great apostle Paul himself had groaned that one! (But *he* went straight on to shout the glorious answer.) 'If we say we have no sin, Lord, we deceive ourselves,' he prayed in the midweek meeting. 'Amen!' chorused the rest of the congregation in the loudest outbreak of fervour that he had ever heard from them. And because his 'wretchedness' was not of the brash and embarrassing type he eventually settled into the mould, accepting his inner conflict, as his fellow-believers had earlier made a pact of peaceful coexistence with their own inconsistencies.

Having another go. Although by such doctrinal excuses he managed to maintain an unsettled truce with his conscience, deep in his heart Lawson really longed to become the more-than-conqueror that God planned he should be. Challenging convention addresses stirred him up to aim for a better quality of life. And in the biographies of the great men of God he saw new hope. The answer to all his spiritual problems lay in discipline, especially in 'the inner closet', he felt sure. So on January 1st he began afresh. He was sleeping reasonably lightly, unconsciously tingling with expectation when the alarm started to ring. He washed and dressed in no time at all and was soon at confession-with-thanksgiving. Next he got down to intercession for others, hopping off at all the world's trouble spots! Ah, this was it: he felt quite fulfilled. Until he looked at his watch. Had he only been going five minutes? Not quite George Whitfield or Praying Hyde! Picking up his Bible he tried to squeeze some meaning out of it, but the going was tough. He began to analyse what might be wrong, assuming a blockage of sin must be somewhere.

Enter the accuser of the brethren who had been standing in the wings; (he had no need of an alarm clock!). 'Obviously you cannot love God very much, Lawson, if you flag after a few minutes of prayer and Bible study.' 'Indeed, I begin to wonder if I am saved at all,' moans our son of the law.

The road ahead divides at this stage for our average pilgrim. He will either drop out of the tradition altogether, or he will flog himself still further. If he chooses the second course the route will go via camps, houseparties and conferences, where he will attempt further fresh starts, intending to really get on with it this time, or at least impress the others with his spirituality. If you object that we are drawing an extreme picture, we can but reply that we really grieve over the many keen disciples of Jesus now ensnared in unnecessary condemnation and moral impotence. We have not exaggerated in describing the bondage that grips many known personally to us. By drawing your attention to the worst cases we hope to set you thinking of the many more known to you, probably yourself included, in whom the pernicious disease of 'Gospel legalism' is less obviously at work.

Zeal without knowledge. Our young friend went off-beam when he reckoned he could do something for God. Although told by his pastor that he'd never been able to fulfil the Ten Commandments, he had accepted the regular bombardments of additional human commandments: 'Read the Bible every day,' 'Pray first thing in the morning;' 'Get your hair cut;' 'Say grace before meals;' 'Get out and witness;' 'Never drink alcohol.' He feared to disregard these unchangeable laws lest he should make himself unspiritual. Failing to keep them, or finding no inward joy when he did succeed to conform outwardly, he just had to dedicate, re-dedicate and at the Annual Whatever, re-rededicate his life to the Lord in the hope of eventually achieving the higher plane of holiness which God will accept. What a distortion of the good news!

With the passing of time he unquestioningly accepted these traditions as fixed principles based on Scripture. All too soon he found himself *keeping all the traditions and breaking God's law of liberty instead of keeping the law and breaking with tradition.* This process turns saints into sinners, but seemingly respectable sinners, and for that very reason worse than unconverted sinners!

Jesus crashed through the respectable fence of the religious niceties of his day. But how do our cautious lives compare with his radical life-style? For that matter, how do we visualize our God? Unconsciously we believe in his middle-class status, his speaking with a nice English accent, his never raising his voice over spiritual matters, his reading only from the King James Version of the Bible, his appreciating Beethoven, and certainly his being the founder member of our denomination! Worshipping such an image has moulded us into it's likeness: traditionally pious, dogmatically cautious, saturated in sentiment and deadly calm in all congregational activities. Certainly not radicals who disturb the status quo as Jesus did.

5. A Test Case

We rock the orthodox boat when we flout the well-established traditions of men as our Master did. But we will get ourselves thrown overboard into the storm like Jonah when we start acting like normal human beings on a Sunday. To pray with our eyes open may be a departure from a human custom, but to play ball, swim, or dig the garden on 'the Lord's day' is surely breaking a commandment of God.

Are you in the L.D.O.S.? At least the Seventh Day Adventists appear to be consistent on this point by observing Saturday as their weekly religious period for inactivity. But the Lord's Day Observance Society have written the *first* day of the week into that fourth commandment. The only mention of the term Lord's Day in Scripture[4] describes the glory of a particular day (perhaps a Tuesday or a Friday) when the sovereign Lord Jesus displayed His majesty and His triumphant purposes to His exiled servant John during His lonely internment on Patmos.

But neither L.D.O.S. or S.D.A. understand the liberation from law that God has granted us in the new covenant. Do our beloved brethren in these camps circumcise their baby boys on the eighth day of their lives and offer regular animal sacrifices in a temple building? To do so would be truly consistent! Now, God has stated his mind on the matter with crystal clarity in Paul's letters to the Galatian and Colossian churches. In both these regions the believers had deviated into heresy. Their warped gospel insisted: 'You need Christ plus feasts, sabbaths, and other holy days.' Thus they equated Christianity with reformed Judaism—quite falsely. The modern emphasis on the recognition of Sundays, Easter, Christmas and other dates as special holy days is a similar crippling of pure Gospel liberty. Many of the early Christians appear to have escaped this Galatian/Colossian half-breed religion. We learn this from the writings of Justin, one of the church fathers, in the account of his dialogues with Trypho, a critic of the believer's way of life. In his first charge against Christians Trypho refers to their wicked abuse of the sabbath. 'This is what we are most at a loss about: that you, professing to be pious, and supposing yourselves better than others, are not in any particular way separated from them, and do not alter your mode of living from the natives, in that you observe no festivals or sabbaths, and do not have the rite of circumcision; and, further, resting your hopes on a man that was crucified you yet expect to obtain some good things from God, while you do not obey his commandments ... Have you not read that the soul shall be cut off from his people who shall not have been circumcised on the eighth day?'

In fact the saints normally worked on Sundays with the rest of the labouring world until Emperor Constantine set Sunday apart as the official 'holy-day' in 321 A.D.

God bound Israel to his law at Sinai. But he never imposed a special national day on any Gentile people as the L.D.O.S.

insists on the religious British Sunday for the entire populace. Paul was referring to himself and his fellow-nationals as Jews when he wrote, 'The law has become *our* tutor to lead *us* to Christ, that *we* may be justified by faith. But now that faith has come, *we* are no longer under a tutor.'[5]

Or are you in continual rest? Although Jesus openly disparaged the rules and regulations of the Pharisees, he carefully kept all the ceremonial requirements of Moses' law—circumcision, turtle-doves, passover, etc. He observed these regulations during his life because the new covenant did not come into force at his birth but at his death and resurrection. He died for the lawless in order to grant forgiveness to the repentant law-breaker. Then he rose and ascended to heaven to fill the pardoned outlaw with the Spirit of Christ. *Since Calvary and pentecost Christ is not only the law-giver, but also the law-keeper within the believer.* 'For to me, to live is Christ.'[6]

Having thoroughly dealt with sin and Satan, Jesus, as the mediator of this better covenant, set a higher law in motion for all who have repented from *dead* works.

'For the law of the Spirit of *life* in Christ Jesus has freed you from the law of sin and death.'[7]

It is life that God has released for His people from Mount Zion, in contrast to the law he issued to Israel from Mount Sinai. Trying to keep the law did not open the Kingdom of God to us; we entered by new birth. Having entered, 'doing certain things' and 'not doing other things' can never make a person spiritual. Paul only referred to sabbaths in order to steer the people of God away from a legalistic attitude towards such 'weak and worthless elemental things'.[8] 'Christ has redeemed us from the curse of the law,' he affirms with triumph:[9] so 'why do you take the slightest notice of those purely human prohibitions?'[10]

Salvation begins with reconciliation, not regulations.

Salvation thrives on life, not laws.

It is true that the apostles visited the synagogue on a Saturday.[11] Not that they felt under law to worship God on that day. But because Jews worshipped at that time of the week they took advantage of this opportunity to preach the Gospel and to reason with their hearers about Jesus' being the Messiah foretold in their scriptures.

The New Testament believers met *every* day for praise, worship and ministry. In this way they observed a seven-day-a-week spiritual sabbath as taught in Hebrews, chapters three and four. That each human body needs one day's rest in seven we fully agree. But there is no divine statute to specify which of the seven. Too many devoted evangelicals are physically and mentally overworked on Sunday! And very few congregations in fact spend much time in actual worship on the first day of the week anyway. They abound in preaching, teaching, testimonies, studies, Sunday school and discussions. Official worship—expressed in song, speech, and quiet contemplation—would barely clock up more than a total of twenty minutes. And much of that would hardly rate as real worship by Old Testament standard of lyre-accompanied song with dance punctuated with hand-clapping and shouts of joy, and interspersed with prostrations and awe-filled silences. We agree that God in sovereign grace often blesses us in our legalistic routine. But let us not draw the false conclusion that our restrictive practices merit his blessings!

'Christ is the end of the law for righteousness to everyone that believeth.'[12] The Greek word 'end' implies that Christ, living in us, expounds the true glory and ultimate *meaning* of the literal commandments. 'Do not think that I have come to do away with the law of Moses and the teaching of the prophets. I have come . . . to give them real meaning.'[13] To limit our behaviour to a literal sabbath-keeping can only stifle the dynamic hidden within that fourth commandment. The Spirit of Christ in us, as in the early disciples, causes sabbath-observance to burst out of the swaddling bands of law into the joyous spiritual freedom of grace.

Absolute rest? Each of us needs to take a long honest look at our regular programme of Christian 'hectivity'. By far the majority of God's dear children who sing and teach pure Gospel facts 'seem to come short of God's rest'.[14] The symptoms of this 'evil-heart-of-unbelief'[15] show up particularly during crisis days. Because of the present outpouring of God's Spirit many of us have received 'the left foot of fellowship' from our church leaders who say they are determined to keep their congregations 'non-charismatic'. Overnight we find ourselves relieved of all offices, and no longer under the pressures of having to preach, teach and organize. But instead of enjoying the God-given rest we feel increasingly guilty about 'doing so much nothing'! Our minds are distracted with the driving temptation to start up another Sunday school or some new club or other.

We are writing out of personal experience: we ourselves had to resist this sense of false guilt in positive faith. Sure, we had often preached about the loveliness of Mary's sitting at Jesus' feet and the wretchedness of Martha's neurotic overwork . . . about the disciples' sense of unbelief while Jesus slept in the storm . . . and about Jesus' allowing Lazarus to die because he loved that sick man and his two sisters who had sent the distress signal. But now that God was asking us to translate our theory into practical behaviour which most of our Christian friends would misinterpret, we frantically hoped he would tell us to hold coffee mornings or launch a visitation programme to justify our spiritual standing. After some really practical lessons in the school of God we 'learned to be content in whatever state' we were.[16]

6. The Vital Key

Now, many of our readers will fear that this gospel—Paul knew no other[17]—will produce undisciplined chaos. 'Should the behaviour of the church resemble that of a Leftist demonstration?' you ask. Indeed not. Nor should it have the symmetry of the cemetery either! 'Are we to continue in sin that grace might increase?' Paul asked when some suggested that his message encouraged licence. Quick as a flash he offers his staccato answer: 'May it never be.'[18] But he did not cease to preach free grace even though he realized that carnal men might indulge their lusts by presuming on God's abounding grace.

How, then, are we to achieve the healthy balance between the carefree enjoyment of the grace of God and the awe produced by the fear of God? Christian bookshops abound in literature on the fear of God: subjects like discipline, fasting, correction, order, church life are readily available. But we can find few titles explaining the other side. Immediately we proclaim pure grace, almost every fundamental believer feels it his bounded duty to 'balance' it up with teaching on discipline, but that of a self-made brand rather than fruit of the Spirit.

Sure, we must exercise discipline. Each of the writers finds this when he returns home to his wife and children after any length of time, having been speaking abroad for example. The telephone keeps ringing, the doorbell works overtime, the desk groans under a pile of unanswered mail and the 'phone pad overflows with umpteen scribbled messages. How does he tackle this challenge? He gets out of ear-shot of the telephone, shuts the office door and tells no-one he is home until he has spent time with his wife and family. Not that he grits his teeth to sweat it out with some sort of I-had-better-do-this-or-my-marriage-will-collapse attitude. The simple secret is that he loves his wife and children. *Love produces the fruit of true discipline; external stoicism manufactures order,* but *a dull and barren order.* 'There is a way which seems right to men, but its end is the way of death.'[19] We preach this readily to the unregenerate church-goer.

Let us not overlook its forceful application to the I'm-trying-to-be-a-better-Christian fellow. Someone will say, 'All right. I agree that we must deliberately take action to overthrow human traditions. And we ought to positively break from the limitation of the shackles of Old Testament literalism about the sabbath. But the New Testament epistles ooze with practical rulings about public prayer, care of widows, modesty of dress, conduct in home and office: they are even called commandments now and again!'[20] Quite correct, but we must understand that the trying Christian makes laws not only from religious traditions and obsolete Old Testament commands, but even makes laws out of the known will of God. 'I've got to love my wife because the Bible says I must.' How ghastly! Obeying the government, honouring his parents, serving his boss, and stewarding money, are treated as an external legislation that threatens his security. He works out a neat scheme of 'thou shalts' and 'thou shalt nots' as his standard of life. But God's standard remains intangible. Christ himself is our norm; to aim at any goal less than *Him* is to sin and fall short of the glory of God.

Dressing modestly, breaking bread weekly, witnessing daily, could all be accomplished by a man's sheer willpower and sacrifice, or just by his natural temperament. He can acquire a religious agility like the fellow on the television who can keep forty plates all spinning on forty sticks. A little wiggle of the prayer stick here, a spin on the study rod there, and a quick flick of the wrist in tract distribution elsewhere—and the show continues its lifelong spin. This man, by substituting 'trying' for 'trusting' runs the risk of turning the whole of his life into a mobile disaster area. Having pictured in his mind some outward pattern for the stated will of God he sets out to implement this vision without the motivating surge of love.

Love for the Lord will produce true discipline in the fear of God. But how do I acquire love? 'We love because He first loved us.'[21] I must keep myself in the love of God, deliberately basking in the warm realization that a most holy God wants for himself this hopeless and unworthy wretch of a fellow, saturating my heart with the sheer bliss of it all. The undeserved goodness of God led Peter the fisherman to repentance. On seeing the colossal haul of fish he dropped down awestruck at Jesus' feet confessing himself to be a sinful man. The grace of God had produced the fear of the Lord!

7. Falling from Grace

The devil will challenge the grace of God right down the line. As a Christian either I believe that God loves me as He loves Jesus and has fully forgiven me every sin and cleansed me thoroughly from all my guilt through Jesus' blood or else I believe that I must earn His love and struggle to please Him by dedicating, sacrificing and labouring. I must know that I was given the royal status of a son of God on being born of His Spirit, or else I must strive to grow into sonship by good deeds. I will thankfully live in the quiet confidence that the Spirit of God is changing me into the likeness of Christ, or else I must ever restlessly pray that God will hitch on some extra virtues. Faith in the faithfulness of my God enables me to walk in unbroken fellowship with Him, so that He can work His own perfect work in my life.

Now, failure to appreciate this goodness

of God sends me back into legalism. This is the devil's foul intention. He sowed doubt about God's pure goodness in the hearts of Adam and Eve; and in dire ingratitude they rebelled against their loving creator. And if I do not accept that the Gospel is as good as Scripture describes it, I will treat every precious command of Christ as deadly law. However, if I follow the leading of the Spirit I will perform these commands in a wholesome way, not under law.[22]

'Go into all the world and preach the Gospel to all creation.'[23] This directive will be carried out because we have fallen in love with the Son of God and thrill through and through with his salvation, or it will become a killing law that *ought* to be performed because Jesus said so. Have you honestly got a burden for souls? Few believers will frankly admit that they have no such burden. They are afraid they would shock their brethren by confessing its absence but they still bash on, preaching the gospel of grace under law!

Paul, who reached and rescued vast numbers of lost sinners, had just one aim in life—overwhelmed by God's love, in deep gratitude, he passionately longed that

'I might know him.'[24] Orthodoxy, having banned passion and looked askance at emotional prayers as signs of immaturity, has even turned *that* Scriptural desire into another statute! 'Are you getting to know him?' pants the preacher. 'How?' the condemned listeners secretly ask themselves. Maybe, 'Read more of the Word', is offered as the prescribed method. 'I can't seem to get anything out of it: in fact I'm not able to read my Bible,' one young man told a colleague of ours at a conference. The average 'counsellor' would have probed for secret sins or suggested a Bible reading aid. But our friend discerned this man's problem. He was under a legal bondage about *having* to read his Bible. Yet New Testament disciples had no personal Bibles with which to have a traditional Quiet Time! Wisely he bid him to give it up for a while. Next day we saw him reading it fervently. Blessed by divine grace he had now developed an appetite for the good book.

Augustine formulated the principle into a pithy saying: 'Love God and do as you please.'

8. Can't I Help a Bit?

'Hold it!' We hear many readers say at this stage. 'Isn't it better that the believer presses on with his witnessing and devotional exercises under law than not at all?'

Well, consider Abraham and his two sons and draw your own conclusions. A son at his time of life? Yes, God had said it[25] so he should just have continued to live a normal life of intimate fellowship with Sarah his wife. But impatience and doubt drove him to the innovation of sleeping with Hagar. She represents legalism—trying to please God.

God granted each woman a son. Tension developed between the two mothers and the two lads. Then God ordered the solution: 'Drive out the bondwoman and her son, for the son of the bondwoman shall not be an heir with the son of the free woman.'[26]

By analogy 'We are not children of the bondwoman (i.e. legalism) but of the free-woman (i.e. grace).'[27]

Attempting to perform the will of God by human determination breeds tension. The modern Middle East conflict stems from Abraham's original helping God out!

9. You Will Get a Summons

We will answer your objection further. Have you considered that God will bring every believer to judgement? *We will be judged by the law of liberty!* And what question will Christ pose to us then? He will ask 'What liberty did you derive from my completed work? With what liberty did you display salvation to the world?' Perhaps many Old Testament saints will find it more tolerable in that day than some of us. 'So speak and so act, as who are to be judged by the law of liberty.'[28]

'One who looks intently at *the perfect law of liberty and abides by it,* not having become a forgetful hearer, but an effective *doer,* this man shall be blessed in what he does.'[29] Disregard for this 'law of liberty', also called 'the law of the Spirit of life in Christ Jesus', leaves one under the gravitational pull of the law of death[7] resulting in dead 'good' works, ideas, plans and pressures.

10. Don't be so Trying?

Do you try really hard not to murder? No, of course not, for that's about the one commandment most of us keep without a conscious thought or effort. But Jesus ripped from us our outward façade of respectability when he said 'Everyone who is angry with his brother shall be guilty before the supreme court.'[30]

Evidently, judging by many Christian conversations, few followers of Christ really take their Master's words seriously. For all their good intentions still they cannot prevent the outbursts of anger towards their husbands, wives, children, teachers business colleagues and fellow-believers. Has God asked for the impossible? Surely not!

Similarly, 'You shall not commit adultery' presents little problem to the majority of God's true children, even in our permissive generation. But Jesus' assessment that 'every one who looks on a woman to lust for her has committed adultery with her already in his heart'[31] leaves not one man smiling with a clear conscience.

39

11. Who's Doing the Work?

'I'm getting confused,' some of you are gasping. 'If I just let myself go and really break free from Moses' law, what's going to happen? I'll keep losing my temper, waste valuable time on carnal trash, huddle up exclusively with my own little clique, and criticize the world and my wife . . . to start with!'

Of course you will, because in your flesh operates an unwritten law that resembles the earth's law of gravity. Scripture calls this spiritual force 'the law of sin and death'.[7] When the flesh is given free rein it produces a sordid assortment of dead works: 'Now the deeds of the flesh are evident: which are immorality, impurity, sensuality, idolatry, sorcery, enmities, strife, jealousy, outbursts of anger, disputes, dissentions, factions, envying, drunkenness, carousing, and things like these.'[32] Most of us could give expression to *all* of these 'works of the flesh' in just one evening without much effort. So how should we cope with these menacing outgrowths of self-centredness?

Most Christians have just one answer:

curb 'the works of the flesh' by 'works of the law'.[33] Now, both sets of works are equally dead and need to be repented of.[34] For 'works of the law' can only produce one thing—a better quality of corpse! The prodigal son gave vent to filthy works of the flesh— (works of *indulgence*)—ending up as a stinking spiritual corpse among the pig-troughs. But, on the other hand, his older brother controlled his flesh by 'works of the law'— (works of *inhibition*) —making himself a sweetly embalmed spiritual mummy—equally dead! Now he was as much company for Father as his runaway younger brother: life eternal is to *know* the Father and Jesus Christ whom He sent into the world.[35] Therefore a tension resulted like that between Ishmael and Isaac.

Indeed, it is preferable to curb the flesh rather than let it run riot—for the good of society. 'Law is not made for the righteous man, but for the lawless and rebellious, for the ungodly and sinners, for the unholy and profane, for those who kill their fathers and mothers, for murderers and immoral men and homosexuals and kidnappers and liars and perjurers and whatever else is contrary to sound teaching.'[36] However, the law can *not* create life.

Do you see that?

But God has set in motion a law of life that conquers our inbred tendency to selfishness. He refuses to improve the flesh; he has sentenced it to crucifixion.[37] Yes, it requires self-control to keep the flesh on the cross; but even that is a fruit of the Spirit.[38]

Grace delivers us from both the indulgent 'works of the flesh', and the inhibiting 'works of the law' by producing within us the 'works of God'—works of *inspiration*.

Jesus, our true standard of living, testified that he operated by this law of life. Therefore his works belonged to neither category of 'dead works'. 'The words I say to you I do not speak of my own initiative'—remember how Ishmael started —'but the Father abiding in me does *His works*.'[39] And when the crowds asked him what they should do so that they too could perform 'the works of God' he taught them the same principle: 'This is the work of God, that you believe in him whom He has sent.'[40]

In other words, we must cease from doing *our own works* in order to enter God's rest.[41]

12. I Give Up

Throughout these pages we have been relentlessly excavating the foundations of a standard 'evangelical' life. By now many a reader is gasping, 'Leave me alone. I feel exposed and insecure under the onslaught of all your digs.' Bear with us as we make this final probe; just ask yourself in fact if you *do* live evangelically, for the very word evangelical implies full acceptance of the good news of free grace. You may with your mind adhere tenaciously to fundamentalist doctrine, but in actual practice run your entire life on a fundamentally wrong principle. By applying a corrective set of laws (legislative statutes) to the flesh in the form of a mild dose of autosuggestion, you can curb and mould your external behaviour into a decent lifestyle that resembles good Christian practice.

But the flesh lusts and hates, covets and lies, envies and criticizes because of the law (motivating principle) of sin and death.

43

The only law that can lick that power hollow is the law of grace! 'The law of the Spirit of life in Christ Jesus has set you free from the law of sin and death!'" just as the liberating law of aerodynamics sets the skylark free from the law of gravity. So, 'Walk by the spirit and you will not carry out the desire of the flesh.'[42] And do let us take care not to line up the cart before the horse as if God ever said, 'Crucify the flesh and you will get into the Spirit.' Rather, we are invited to set the heart before the course: 'If by *the Spirit* you are putting to death the deeds of the body, you will live.'[43] No evangelical ever actually recites that Reversed Version, but the majority appear to govern their lives by such a rule of thumb.

13. Mind the Trap

May God have mercy on us as we resolve to rise up and really live by the Spirit. For, no sooner do we decide to walk in the Spirit free from religious laws ('rules') and the law of sin and death ('pulls') than we sense new pressures upon us due to pentecostal laws (more 'rules'). Without doubt

the so-called charismatic renewal represents the main thrust in God's progressive
work in these days. But even in this move-
ment some ministers lay down the unscriptural law of 'tarrying for the Spirit'.
As a result, our young friend Lawson has
to earn baptism in the Spirit as before he
was made to work hard to earn his baptism
in water. Then 'Bye-law No. 2' declares,
'You must speak in tongues to prove to us
that you are filled with the Spirit', which
can hardly claim to be grace! The 'have-
nots' in Lawson's set become defensive and
nervy because they do not speak in
tongues; they have never been told the
good news that God grants the ability to
speak with tongues as the blessed *con-
sequence* of baptism in the Spirit and *not*
as dogmatic *evidence*.

If in child-like trust Lawson accepts
simply and sweetly the glorious grace-gift
of the Holy Spirit he can begin to worship
God in a new language. Thereupon he
plunges joyously into the freedom of life
in the Spirit, blissfully ignorant of the
pseudo-spiritual laws with which his
friends will lead him in the days ahead.
For instance, some enthusiasts in his
charismatic group will look him in the eye

as they forcefully proclaim, 'Jesus is won-
derful! Hallelujah!' Maybe his spirit is
subdued due to a prayer-burden, but as
his friends exclaim 'Praise the Lord' with
such exuberance he feels a cloud of condemnation settle on his heart because he
cannot respond with equal volume. Using
such expressions as an external tempera-
ture gauge of other people's spiritual
warmth pressurizes them under a law of
the most deceptive kind.

James cautions all such law-enforcement
officers, 'Let not many of you become
teachers, my brethren, knowing that as
such we shall incur a stricter judgement,'[44]
and Jesus counsels them 'Do not judge lest
you be judged yourselves.'[45] The fear of
such men will ensnare you.[47] All too many
'charismatic' elders and pastors hold the
flock in legal bondage because they themselves live in fear of the judgement of their
peers. But let us say categorically that so
long as you walk in the Spirit in harmony
with God's complete revelation of his mind
in the Scriptures, you need not feel guilty
for failing to fit the popular pattern. Live
unto God and not unto men,[46] for he is
your judge. And remember that His
standard is the perfect law of liberty as

exemplified in the many-faceted life of Jesus.

Self-opinionated religious bigots detest liberty. Jesus did not submit to the pharisees of his day. So why should you endure the strait-jacket existence demanded of you by their modern counterparts? The law of man working through the law of death produces strife and hurt, fears and confusion, impatience and bitterness, apathy and every other neurotic symptom. But the law (ruling principle of conduct) of life promotes righteousness and radiance, compassion and submission, liberty and wholesomeness.

14. Will I Offend?

This is the devil's trump card to keep the saints in their shells. Professing Christians who resist this pure message of grace played that card right at the start and so shut their ears to all that we have been saying. But even those of our readers who have found help in the fore-going pages to surmount one obstacle of doubt and fear after another will be tempted to draw back right here. In answer we beg of you to distinguish carefully between two categories of people who will be stumbled. The pharisees *need* to be offended because their false gospel is hindering many a man of the world from accepting the true gospel of God. Jesus, in his compassion for the sick and suffering and in obedience to his loving Father, often healed deliberately on the Sabbath, thereby annoying his hypocritical opponents. However, if my free behaviour would stumble a weaker brother's conscience so that he gets lost,[48] I can trust the Spirit of Christ to prompt me to sacrifice my liberty with a view of saving him—and that means winning him over eventually to the joy of freedom also.

One of the writers knows a wealthy Christian family who always drank a little wine with every meal. When a drunkard, newly converted came to live with them they locked away their entire stock of wine and refrained from even the mention of the subject out of loving consideration for their weaker brother. After several weeks had elapsed they poured out a white wine during one supper, then let some dry days pass before introducing the beverage again. Ultimately the new member of the household had developed sufficient strength and confidence in the Lord to freely share in their regular meal-time practice. Such caring ministry built him up in his inner man till he became mature and knew he was free. Had they regularly thrust alcohol upon him from the beginning it could have driven him straight back to his former bondage. On the other hand, to have continued to practice unbroken teetotalism over the years in their home could have left him with a lurking life-long fear that at a weak moment in some future worldly business meeting he might accept a 'fatal draught'.

Should a brother who is really sold out to Jesus wish to have a drink at the 'local', mow his lawn on a Sunday morning, or relax on the beach with an ice-cream on Sunday afternoons, the New Testament tells him to feel utterly free to do so. 'Oh, but what a bad witness', we hear some respectable Christians exclaiming. Witness? If done with a clear conscience before God it could be a grand witness to Gospel liberation. Those who do so object also propound the equally crazy notion that their method of water-baptism demonstrates a good testimony to the world—when performed ceremoniously in

the seclusion of some special building!
Come, come. Let us burst forth from these
God-dishonouring grave-clothes of human
sentimentality.

15. Why Bend Over Backwards?

No honest reader will deny that the
apostle Paul lived out his life in untram-
melled Gospel liberty. He burned with the
determination that no Gentile convert
should ever be forced to practice any Old
Testament ritual; so much so that he could
deliver such blistering speeches that would
fairly scorch off the ears of anybody who
compromised. In his letter to the Galatians
he quotes two typical incidents.

Referring to an interview with men of
repute in the church in Jerusalem he
records that 'Titus, Greek though he is,
was not compelled to be circumcised. That
course was urged only as a concession to
certain sham Christians, interlopers who
had stolen in to spy upon the liberty we
enjoy in the fellowship of Christ Jesus.
These men wanted to bring us into bondage, but not for one moment did I yield
to their dictation; I was determined that

the full truth of the Gospel should be maintained for you.'[49]

The other example of Paul's outspoken attack on compromise occurred when Peter visited Antioch. 'I opposed him to his face, because he was clearly in the wrong. For until certain persons came from James he was taking meals with Gentile Christians; but when they came he drew back and began to hold aloof, because he was afraid of the advocates of circumcision. The other Jewish Christians showed the same lack of principle; even Barnabas was carried away and played false like the rest. But when I saw that their conduct did not square with the truth of the Gospel, I said to Cephas (Peter) before the whole congregation, "If you, a Jew born and bred, live like a Gentile, and not like a Jew, how can you insist that Gentiles must live like Jews?" '[50]

But Paul was never 'in bondage to his freedom'. He held himself free to sacrifice this New Testament liberty of his. Luke describes in his journal what happened on a later trip to Jerusalem. 'Next day Paul paid a visit to James; we were with him, and all the elders attended. He greeted them, and then described in detail all that

God had done among the Gentiles through his ministry. When they heard this, they gave praise to God. Then they said to Paul: "You see, brother, how many thousands of converts we have among the Jews, all of them staunch upholders of the law. Now they have been given certain information about you: it is said that you teach all the Jews in the Gentile world to turn their backs on Moses, telling them to give up circumcising their children and following our way of life. What is the position, then? They are sure to hear that you have arrived. You must therefore do as we tell you. We have four men here who are under a vow; take them with you and *go through the ritual of purification with them,* paying their expenses, after which they may shave their heads. Then everyone will know that there is nothing in the stories they were told about you, but that you are a practising Jew and keep the law yourself." '[51]

How should Paul respond to this request? Surely, to be consistent, he must refuse to take part in this scheme: so says the law of outward conformity. But as a man of the Spirit, Paul was led to curtail his freedom and to submit to the leadership of the Church where he was the guest. An admirable and commendable attitude of heart. Foregoing his liberty he attended the temple and practised Old Covenant rites. Similarly the present writers have from time to time accepted restricted schedules and formal customs while ministering in traditional churches.

But we must squarely face the sixty-four thousand dollar question: Did the elders' plan succeed? Was their desire to cause no offence to the Jews fulfilled? Definitely not. Instead they brought down about their ears a colossal disaster. The violent mob, completely misinterpreting Paul's action and suspicious of his motive, beat him and clamoured for his blood. The temple courts seethed with turmoil, reverberating with the hubbub of their yells of 'Kill him! Kill him!'[52]

Admittedly, God overruled the elders' 'good idea', turning this folly to Paul's advantage. Because Paul loved him, God worked all these things together for his ultimate good, giving him the opportunity to witness before notable dignitaries including the emperor.

However, as for the Church leaders' concern to maintain the status quo in the temple routine, God had other plans. He demolished the entire 'old order' a few years later.

Many of our readers right now face some parallel dilemma. We offer no law of 'Come out' or 'Stay in'. We plead with you to co-operate with the undercurrent of the River of God in your deepest heart: that is the only safe course. But be ruthlessly honest with yourself, or else you will be victimized by group pressures. In your ultimate decision do you resemble those nervous Jerusalem elders or the heart-at-peace Paul? Our hearts cry to God to

Raise up a people holy and free;
Hearts with a vision like unto Thee;
Souls that would rather die than give in;
Lives with a passion victory to win.
Set all our hearts ablaze with Thy love,
Teach us the secret of life from above.

16. What Does Jesus Want of Us?

That wine-drinking European family gave expression to the power and wisdom of a loving God in redeeming a ruined member of His creation. They were fully expounding the law, 'for the whole law is fulfilled in one word, in the statement: You shall love your neighbour as yourself'.[53]

As we truly appreciate the Calvary love of our gracious Lord Jesus, we love him in return, longing with all our heart to please him in every way. 'If you love me you will keep my commandments,'[54] He said. Whereas the old covenant law demanded 'You must', Jesus' new commandments promise that 'You will'. These promises are issued under guarantee to every believing believer who will accept them. Drop your old name Lawson, for we are not children of law but children of promise. Take on your honourable title of Freeman, for you were not born of the will of man (which is law),[55] but God has begotten you by his own will[56] and works into you both the willingness and ability to do of His good pleasure.[57] Oh, hear the gladsome note of the trump of jubilee in the fourth verse of Ryden's hymn, 'Buried with Christ'—that delightful metrical version of the sixth chapter of the Epistle to the Romans:

Not under law, I'm now under grace,
Sin is dethroned and Christ takes its place.

The law had told me how often I had miserably sinned, but the Gospel assures me that 'grace abounded all the more'.[58] Yet even the law never showed me the full extent of my mess. Need I ever know it? But I have no doubt that Christ displaced my accumulated sins at Calvary, and now replaces the menacing magnetic pull of sin in my flesh.

Well, what does Jesus require of me? What are his commandments. To love God, to love my neighbour as (thirdly) I love myself.[59]

Very few Christians really love them-*selves*. No wonder, then, that they are critical and cold towards their neighbours. I am worth a lot to my heavenly Father— valued at the price of Jesus' blood. I am forgiven and cleansed and made worthy to be called a son of God because he has accepted me in the Beloved. I am a new self, for 'it is no longer I who live, but Christ lives in me'.[60] I must not despise this new 'me', this life I live by faith in the Son of God and by obedience to the inward urge of the law of the Spirit. Rather, I will honour and respect you, young Free- man.

When I realize that God's Son did not

take on the nature of angels to die for the salvation of demons, but became a man for us men and our redemption, I cannot help but love and respect my fellow-*men* recognizing the potential that God sees in them.

And when I see what the true and living *God* is really like, instead of visualizing his man-made caricatured effigy, how can I help but love him?

17. Rise Up and Take the Kingdom

No doubt a number of theologians among our readers feel that this little book has an *anti-nomian* emphasis, (which, by interpretation, means 'against law'). We emphatically disagree: we have in fact written a truly evangelical *a-nomian* treatise (meaning 'no law'). For when the believer properly fulfils the law he renders it obsolete.

Why have we persisted in ferreting down every religious rabbit-hole we could think of? Not because we set ourselves up as a pair of 'dropped-out' critics who have nothing better to do than vent our cynical frustrations on Christendom. Rather, we burn with a consuming longing to see a victorious generation of overcomers march forth in perfect freedom in the Spirit to 'bring the King back'.[61]

This will never be achieved by a crowd of anarchists each doing what is right in his own eyes. The generation we seek will experience the strong discipline of their much-loved Master. Free from all external rules, but inwardly prompted and enabled by the Spirit of truth, they will translate into a full range of rhythm, tempo, keys and volume the perfect rhapsody of God's law. By comparison the limping rule-keepers will sound as flat and pedantic as legal documents! Nehemiah emerged from the cosiness of Babylonian exile in order to restore the old waste places of Zion in readiness for the promised King. Who offered the major opposition to this work of recovery? Not Gentile pagans, but half-breed people who all claimed some family link with Abraham. How did he handle the situation? He adopted a no-nonsense policy that led to the purging out of the renewed nation every case of mixed marriages and expelling every foreign infiltration from the work of God.

Paul faced a parallel problem in his

task of foundation-laying in Galatia.

The trouble did not now lie in mixed marriages and tribal interchange because the new covenant had annulled all racial and social distinctions such as Jew and Gentile, Greek and Barbarian, freeman and slave. In this case the hindrances arose through spiritual half-castes who introduced a mixture of legalism into the pure Gospel. These trouble-mongers denied full salvation to Gentile disciples unless they accepted the humiliation of circumcision and the inconvenience of special sacred days.[62] What was Paul's policy towards these 'spiritual Samaritans?' He counselled believers, free born citizens of 'Jerusalem above', (his code-name for grace),[63] to resist them 'Don't yield.'[64] He personally confronted Peter publicly—although he was an honoured leader—when he yielded to their demands.[50] And in some cases he implied tougher measures: 'Cast them out.'[65]

Must we bulldoze over the foibles of our weaker brethren? You may well ask with real concern. What does God wish? If a brother has scruples about vegetarianism and Sabbath-keeping we must welcome him as God has received him but *not for disputes over opinions.*[66] The Lord forbids us pressurizing this man with a law in case that should force him to quit his religious restrictions before he has true faith for full freedom. Of course, the same Scripture equally forbids him using his weaknesses as a drag on the liberty of the community to which he commits himself in fellowship. But, without a shadow of a doubt, *teachers* of legalism must be silenced.

18. They'll Have to Go

'Christ means the end of the struggle for righteousness-by-the-law for everyone who believes in him.'[67] 'Whosoever believes in Him shall not be disappointed.'[68] So rest your entire weight on the grace of God.

'Keep standing firm and do not be subject again to the yoke of slavery,' namely legalism over religious matters.[69] 'Cast out the bondwoman and her son' (every trace of the compulsion and condemnation produced by legalism), 'for the son of the bondwoman shall not be heir with the son of the free woman'.[65] Grace and law will never settle for peaceful co-existence. One must be evicted. Not only the woman but her offspring—all that she produces—

must be thrown out. Away with sentiment. It is time for every genuine believer in Jesus, under His lordship, to turn ruthlessly and without pity on this intruding bond-woman, and tell her plainly and firmly, 'Get out and stay out'.

Then we can yield ourselves up entirely to the surging flow of the Spirit, enjoying a life lived to the praise of the glory of his grace.

Presently, when God's spiritual temple is completed, the innumerable company of us redeemed wretches will shout 'grace, grace' unto it.[70] And long after this present rat-race order of society has finished its history and

We've been there ten thousand years,
Bright shining as the sun,
We've no less days to praise God's *grace,*
Than when we first begun.

'My brethren, you have *died to the law* so that you may belong to . . . him who has been raised from the dead in order that we may bear fruit for God.[71]

'Now we are *discharged from the law,* dead to that which held us captive, so that we may serve, not under the old written code but in the new life of the Spirit.'[72]

61

Scriptural References

All quotations are from the *New American Standard Bible* unless otherwise indicated.

1. Romans 6:14
2. Galatians 5:18
3. Isaiah 12:2
4. Revelation 1:10
5. Galatians 3:24–25
6. Philippians 1:21
7. Romans 8:2
8. Galatians 4:9–10
9. Galatians 3:13
10. Colossians 2:20 (J. B. Phillips)
11. Acts 18:4
12. Romans 10:4 (King James)
13. Matthew 5:17
14. Hebrews 4:1 (King James)
15. Hebrews 3:12 (King James)
16. Philippians 4:11 (Revised Standard)
17. Galatians 1:6–8
18. Romans 6:1–2
19. Proverbs 14:12
20. 1 Corinthians 7:25; 1 Thessalonians 4:2 (King James)
21. 1 John 4:19
22. Romans 8:4
23. Matthew 28:19
24. Philippians 3:10
25. Genesis chapters 15 and 16
26. Galatians 4:30
27. Galatians 4:31
28. James 2:12
29. James 1:25
30. Matthew 5:22
31. Matthew 5:28
32. Galatians 5:19–21
33. Galatians 2:16 and 3:2,5

34. Hebrews 6:1
35. John 17:3
36. 1 Timothy 1:9–11
37. Galatians 5:24
38. Galatians 5:23
39. John 14:10
40. John 6:28–29
41. Hebrews 4:10 (King James)
42. Galatians 5:16
43. Romans 8:13
44. James 3:1
45. Matthew 7:1
46. Colossians 2:16
47. Proverbs 29:25 (King James)
48. 1 Corinthians 8:13
49. Galatians 2:3–5 (New English Bible)
50. Galatians 2:11–14 (New English Bible)
51. Acts 21:18–24 (New English Bible)
52. Acts 21:27–36
53. Galatians 5:14
54. John 14:15
55. John 1:13
56. James 1:18
57. Philippians 2:13
58. Romans 5:20
59. Mark 12:30–31
60. Galatians 2:20
61. 2 Samuel 19:10–12, 43
62. Galatians 1:6–9
63. Galatians 4:26
64. Galatians 2:5
65. Galatians 4:30
66. Romans 14:1 (Revised Standard)
67. Romans 10:4 (J. B. Phillips)
68. Romans 10:11 (J. B. Phillips)
69. Galatians 5:1
70. Zechariah 4:7
71. Romans 7:4 (Revised Standard)
72. Romans 7:6 (Revised Standard)

More Good Reading . . .
AMAZING GRACE by Maurice Smith 95p
Amazing grace! How sweet the sound that saved a wretch like me. So wrote John Newton, the slave trader, after his conversion. Two hundred and fifty years later it is Maurice Smith's theme tune and his turn to experience . . . amazing grace.

Don't deceive yourself. Everyone's moment of truth arrives sometime. For Maurice it was the realization that grace is God's love in action. And that love itself is more than a vague influence upon our lives: it is a truly liberating factor.

Newton was a slave to sin for much of his life. Yet he ended his days as a country vicar. Maurice Smith's life is no less varied and an equally bumpy ride. As he himself says, it is essentially a book of experiences and he hopes you will not only enjoy it, but also save yourself some pain and learn at his expense in meeting the present-day problems of social status, finance, sex, and the awful bogey of trying to be a good Christian.

Good Reading publications are available from all booksellers. If you have any difficulty, please send the purchase price together with 10p postage for each copy of the book to: Good Reading Ltd, 27 Chancery Lane, London WC2A 1NF.

I enclose a cheque/postal order for ☐ copies of Amazing Grace by Maurice Smith plus 10p per copy to cover postage and packing.

Name ....

Address ....

....